GIG
CX

CUSTOMER SERVICE IN THE TWENTY-FIRST CENTURY

BRIAN PRITCHARD, TERRY RYBOLT &
MARK HILLARY

GigCX: Customer Service In The Twenty-First Century

© Brian Pritchard, Terry Rybolt, and Mark Hillary 2020
All Rights Reserved

Published by LiveXchange Books
Arroyo Grande, California, USA

https://livexchange.com

LiveXchange Books
1375 East Grand Ave, Suite 103 #238
Arroyo Grande,
California 93420
USA

https://livexchange.com

Author portraits all supplied by the authors.

Cover by: Giovanni Misagrande

ISBN: 9798550351123

GigCX: Customer Service In The Twenty-First Century
© Brian Pritchard, Terry Rybolt, and Mark Hillary 2020

The right of Brian Pritchard, Terry Rybolt, and Mark Hillary to be identified as the authors of this work has been asserted by them in accordance with the Copyright, Designs and Patents Act 1988.

All rights reserved. No part of this publication may be reproduced, stored in or introduced into a retrieval system, or transmitted, in any form, or by any means (electronic, mechanical, photocopying, recording, or otherwise) without the prior written permission of the publisher. Any person who does any unauthorized act in relation to this publication may be liable to criminal prosecution and civil claim for damages.

This book is dedicated to everyone who makes the CX industry what it is today - one of the most exciting international industries to be a part of... and with GigCX it's only getting better!

CONTENTS

About The Authors 9
Foreword 15
Preface and Introduction 19

Chapter One: The Gig Economy Is Coming For CX - And Fast! 25

Chapter Two: In-house Or Outsourced CX? Why Not Just Take Control? 29

Chapter Three: The Future Of CX Can Be Found In The Cloud 33

Chapter Four: How To Manage Holiday Staffing In The New Normal 37

Chapter Five: The Future Of Managing Seasonal Spikes In Customer Service 41

Chapter Six : Why Platforms Are The Future For CX 45

Chapter Seven: Work From Anywhere Beats Work From Home 49

Chapter Eight: GigCX Is Coming And It's Better Than Anything You Have Seen 53

Chapter Nine: GigCX Offers A Path To The Future Of Work 57

Chapter Ten: The Gig Economy Transformed The Cost Of Hotels And Taxis - Why Not CX?.........63

Chapter Eleven: How To Smooth Out Seasonality By Taking Control Of CX 67

Chapter Twelve: Using Flexibility To Build CX Resilience 71

Chapter Thirteen: Outsourcing To A BPO Is Not The Only Path To Great CX!..................................75

Chapter Fourteen: Conclusion And Closing Thoughts On GigCX..79

References..87

Appendix 1: LiveXchange as an Enabler of Gig CX 93

ABOUT THE AUTHORS

Brian Pritchard, is based in Toronto, Ontario and is the CEO of LiveXchange. A self-confessed entrepreneurial zealot and fully experienced in the difficult task of bringing new business ideas to successful operational fruition in challenging environments. Brian founded LiveXchange in 2002, long before work at home and gig economy were household terms. One of Brian's key strengths is in leading the cultural and technological changes as a corporation goes remote helping to change and advance the relationship between the corporation and the employee.

http://bit.ly/bpritchard
https://livexchange.com

Terry Rybolt, a 20 year BPO industry veteran, is the Chief Revenue Officer for LiveXchange based in Boston, MA. Terry joined LiveXchange in 2020 after 12 years at Teleperformance serving in numerous executive functions, most recently as Managing Director, overseeing the global work at home go to market strategy for the company.

http://bit.ly/rybolt
https://livexchange.com

M**ark Hillary** is a British technology writer and analyst, based in São Paulo, Brazil. He studied Software Engineering and has an MBA from the University of Liverpool.

Mark hosts the CX Files podcast - a weekly show focused on the future of customer experience. He frequently contributes to the global media, focused on technology and CX, with articles published by the BBC, Financial Times, Reuters, and Huffington Post. He has regular CX-focused columns in Intelligent Sourcing and Engage Customer.

Mark has written several books focused on technology. His first was titled 'Outsourcing to India: The Offshore Advantage' published in 2004 by Springer in Germany. He co-wrote 'Global Services: Moving To A Level Playing Field' with Dr Richard Sykes in 2007 for the British Computer Society and he translated all of Shakespeare's sonnets into tweets for his 2015 book 'My Tweets Are Nothing Like The Sun: William Shakespeare On Twitter.'

Mark has advised several national governments on technology policies and has advised the United Nations on the use of technology for development. He even co-authored a book titled 'Leveraging Social Media for SMEs' in 2013, published by the International Trade Center at the UN.

http://bit.ly/markhillary
http://carnabysp.com
Social: @markhillary

FOREWORD

Customer experience (CX) management is rapidly evolving, and successful organizations will be those that pivot quickly in order to adapt to new realities. No matter the country or the industry, there is more interest among those responsible for managing interactions with consumers to find better ways of driving the best possible outcomes in an efficient, cost-effective fashion.

GigCX is an evolution, an acceptance of what the World Economic Forum in Davos has called the Fourth Industrial Revolution. In short, the traditional way of managing contact centers and agents is finished.

It is in this context that the gig CX technology enabler LiveXchange's solution is relevant to the current contact center marketplace. As customer management decentralizes into agents' homes, there is a premium for one-stop shop capabilities that drive efficiencies and best possible outcomes.

Before the Covid-19 coronavirus pandemic of 2020 many executives were wary of embracing a work from home customer service model, but it has been proven to work successfully. However, the dynamics of managing a contact center should not simply be transplanted into a distributed working environment and this is where GigCX can not only change the rules but allows them to be rewritten.

LiveXchange is positioned at the forefront of the gig CX curve. This book is even a testament to that - there are no other books I can find on Amazon that feature 'GigCX' in the title - the authors have surpassed themselves in delivering this thought leadership ahead of the broader CX marketplace. LiveXchange has effectively replaced generic Customer Relationship Management (CRM) with a solution that is designed for the changing face of customer interactions.

The reality is, today's more entrepreneurial gig delivery environment demands more than legacy CRM systems can offer. We are no longer planning for a workforce that only operates on fixed 4 or 8 hour work periods. The LiveXchange solution allows work to be planned around 30-minute periods, which is relevant for workers planning how and when they can contribute as well as companies that want to drive flexibility and efficiency.

This also allows companies to plan for or react to seasonality problems. Why should Black Friday be a problem when you can just offer hundreds more available shifts on the system?

The gig workforce is more of a factor in customer experience management than anyone could have imagined - especially pre-Covid. Talented and experienced contact center agents, especially those in a virtual setting, are more focused on working in an entrepreneurial fashion. They are generally older and more focused on a specific brand or woman when compared to employees in traditional contact centers.

Forward-looking organizations, including those in the small-and medium-sized category, need to take all this into account. These statements were also quantified in the most recent Ryan Strategic Advisory Front Office BPO Omnibus Survey of contact center executives, in which North American respondents from enterprises of up to $500m in revenues identified gig capabilities as a top 5 key selling point for their suppliers (tied for 5th with omnichannel capabilities).

This clearly demonstrates that GigCX will be an extremely important area within the wider CX industry. Change has taken place at a dramatic pace during 2020. Work from home was embraced, digital transformation has been accelerated, and automation is being rushed into production, but underpinning all these actions the contact center remains - even if it does not look like a traditional contact center.

2021 is not going to look like 2019. The authors of this book are demonstrating here that GigCX is a trend that has been talked about for a long time, but now the time for action has arrived. As the late management expert William Bridges once said in his 1994 book 'JobShift':

> "What is disappearing today is not just a certain number of jobs, but the very thing itself – the job ... [Jobs are a] rigid solution to an elastic problem ... When the work that needs doing changes constantly, we cannot afford the inflexibility that the job brings with it."

GigCX is an idea that has now arrived. The growth of the broader gig economy combined with the work-from-home experience of 2020 has shown that customer service contact centers can be designed in a completely new way. What seemed to be distant is now a part of our present-day reality.

Peter Ryan
Principal Analyst, Ryan Strategic Advisory

Montreal, Canada
October 2020
https://ryanadvisory.com/

PREFACE AND INTRODUCTION

> "Here's to the crazy ones, the misfits, the rebels, the troublemakers, the round pegs in the square holes... the ones who see things differently — they're not fond of rules... You can quote them, disagree with them, glorify or vilify them, but the only thing you can't do is ignore them because they change things..."
>
> —**Steve Jobs, 1997,**
> *"Think Different"*

Why did we write this book together? It's a good question because the gig economy has been around for some time. As Peter Ryan mentioned in his foreword, management thinkers were talking about this back in the 90s. Charles Handy even talked about the future of the portfolio career back in the 80s. What's different now?

The truth is that many changes have taken place gradually, leading to what might be called a perfect storm. Companies like Uber and Airbnb demonstrated that platforms can change the world.

If you connect a service provider to a buyer of services in a flexible way that adds value then you can change an entire industry - who is still stepping out into the street in the rain waving their arm for a taxi?

Cloud-based services that are paid for as they are needed has also become an accepted standard for everything from computer software to language or piano tuition. Paying for what you need and only paying for what you consume, rather than an ongoing license has been normalized.

The Covid-19 pandemic proved that working from home could be safe, secure, and successful. The major contact center companies had only tens of thousands of employees based at home in 2019. This is in an industry that employs millions of customer service agents globally.

After Covid, those companies had to make it work and the success stories have become almost tiring to read because of their frequency - another company proves that it's possible to deliver with agents based at home.

But it's very different to design a solution that expects people to be based from home - rather than an emergency response to a pandemic. If you are designing a flexible home-based service solution then you can widen the net and search for people anywhere.

This means you can hire people who value flexibility. They want to work from home - they have not been forced into this. They want to work from home because they are more entrepreneurial and excited by their work. They want to work flexible hours. They want to work only with brands they like - so you can search for fans of the companies you are supporting.

This combination of the cloud, platforms, and the evolution of work from home operating models means that all the stars are now aligned for GigCX to flourish.

Many executives may still believe that customer service requires a contact center staffed with agents or an outsourced agreement with a contact center company. What if you can just build a virtual contact center in the cloud and manage this as a software platform so agents based at home can login and service your customers as and when required?

if it sounds like an unusual idea then imagine what the boss of Hilton Hotels thought about Airbnb back in 2008? In the midst of a global financial meltdown who would have thought that a platform offering spare rooms to strangers would change the entire hospitality industry?

This is the opportunity presented by GigCX. In this book we will explain the opportunity and how to get started. LiveXchange has been perfecting a GigCX model for almost two decades now so you will find an abundance of ideas inside these pages. It's short and direct - you can probably understand our ideas in just one hour.

If you really want to understand the New Normal for CX then you need to understand where GigCX will take the industry in 2021.

Brian Pritchard
Terry Rybolt
Mark Hillary

October 2020

"If we leave it to professionals themselves to reinvent their workplace, are we asking the rabbits to guard the lettuce?"

—Professor Richard Susskind,
*The Future of the Professions:
How Technology Will Transform the
Work of Human Experts, 2017*

CHAPTER ONE

THE GIG ECONOMY IS COMING FOR CX - AND FAST!

Everyone knows about the gig economy[1]. The popularity of tools such as Uber, Lyft, Doordash, and Airbnb, means that the concept of the gig economy is well known and understood. Around 36% of Americans work inside the gig economy so a lot of people understand it not just because they use Doordash to order dinner, but because it provides their income.

But why don't you hear so much about the gig economy in customer service or customer experience (CX)? When you think of customer service most people immediately think of contact centers, not apps or platforms.

LiveXchange is changing that by focusing on GigCX. What is really important to note about services such as Airbnb or Uber is that they are really platforms[2]. They connect a person who wants to offer a service - the driver - with someone who needs a ride. They add value for both by making it easy to find either a driver OR the next customer.

The LiveXchange platform[3] does exactly the same for customer service. You use the platform to design how you want customers to be supported then the agents can connect and serve your customers. The agents can be anywhere because they are working from home and that allows you to select a group of people for your team that are superior to the traditional model of hiring only those people within commuting distance of a contact center.

If this seems like a radical solution then look at how quickly the gig economy took off in so many other sectors. Here's a few thoughts on some of the advantages of using a gig-based platform solution for customer service:

1. **Expertise:** you can focus far more on getting domain experts, rather than hiring people and training them to support a product they are not even interested in. If you are supporting a video game then you can hire gamers who want to earn some cash supporting other gamers. You are free of the requirement to only hire locally, you can cast the net globally and hire the best experts that know and love your products.

2. **Agility:** does your requirement for customer service come evenly spaced across 8-hour shifts? We don't think so,

so why hire contact center agents and ask them to work 8-hour shifts? The agility you gain from a gig-based approach is that you can make sure more agents are there for the spikes and very few are working when you know it's going to be quiet.

3. **Flexibility:** you want to scale up quickly to cope with Black Friday? No problem, just get more agents on the platform. You want to start supporting a new product next week? No problem, just train your agents and they will be ready. You want to open an entirely new virtual contact center in ten days? No problem, how many people do you need?

4. **Efficiency:** think about the costs involved in running a big contact center. All those costs eventually get charged back to the clients. Why not focus on the only things you really need - a platform and the agents? It's like comparing a taxi company that locks up capital by buying a fleet of cars to Uber.

5. **Resilience:** we know what happened to all the contact centers during the Covid-19 pandemic. They had to send everyone home overnight with a laptop. Not everyone has space to work or even wants to work from home. Now they are struggling to open the contact centers again because of the social distancing rules. Why not just avoid all this

and work with agents who love flexible work they can do from home?

There is increasing evidence that more people want to work this way. Everest Research suggests that by 2025, 75% of the workforce will be Millennials and Gen Z all with an increasing preference for gig working[4]. GigCX is an attractive model for older people who want to supplement retirement income with something flexible they can do from home. This also creates an experienced pool of talent for brands who want to hire agents for domain knowledge, not just the school they attended.

The Everest research also suggests that by 2021, 25% of all contact center agents will be hired via a gig platform. We suspect that this will actually be higher because Everest published their research just before the Covid-19 pandemic. More recent research suggests that GigCX has had an enormously positive impact on the confidence and mental health of agents[5] because they have continued to work and remain productive during the crisis.

However you slice it, GigCX is the future for customer service. Many companies will be exploring better options for their customer service processes after the difficulties experienced during the lockdown. Platforms are the way to go.

CHAPTER TWO

IN-HOUSE OR OUTSOURCED CX? WHY NOT JUST TAKE CONTROL?

When executives are planning how they are going to manage their customer service there is often a focus on one question - do you keep it in-house or outsource it to a customer experience (CX) specialist?

This is a question that has been asked for at least the past couple of decades[1]. A further dimension is whether to offshore the customer service team, whether it's in-house or outsourced. In recent years outsourcing has taken the lead because managing customer service has become so complex. Managing a 24/7 contact center using multiple languages and communication channels isn't easy and is usually better left to the experts.

But what if there were another choice?

Don't outsource the work and pay for all those employees inside a contact center. Just use a cloud-based virtual contact center that you have complete control over from inside your own organization and then train gig workers so you have a pool of agents you can use - as and when required.

This reframes the question. By using a CX platform you don't need to hire in a company that offers specialist CX contact centers. You retain complete control of your customer service processes and all the services you need to manage your virtual contact center are offered within the platform.

If this sounds too good to be true - because you have years in CX management and know how things work - then let's use an analogy from another industry.

If my company needs a large amount of cars to get people around then should we purchase the cars and hire drivers onto our payroll or outsource our transport requirement to a dedicated limo company, or give everyone on our team access to a corporate Uber account?

Which option sounds smarter in the twenty-first century? Which option reduces the need for any capital expenditure and also improves agility?

Retaining control over your contact center by using cloud architecture and gig-based agents offers a number of additional advantages over the in-house and outsourced options too:

1. **Resilience:** your architecture is in the cloud. A fire or earthquake at your office will

never take down your contact center. Your agents are working from home so even if this Covid-19 pandemic takes longer than expected to disappear, it's still business as usual for your team. Build resilience into your future customer service solution.

2. **Flexibility:** you can train a much larger pool of agents than you require on average days and you can control the shifts offered by the system, so you can scale down for quiet periods and scale up quickly for the Holiday sales or Black Friday.

3. **Cost:** you are not paying for contact center employees to be sitting around on 8-hour shifts whether they are busy or not. You just pay for the volume of customer interactions, not for buildings or any other infrastructure. Pay for what you need.

Why not just take control and bring your customer service strategy into the twenty-first century? You don't need to choose between in-house CX or outsourced, you can manage it yourself using a platform.

CHAPTER THREE

THE FUTURE OF CX CAN BE FOUND IN THE CLOUD

Cloud architecture has been growing in popularity for a long time now. Google Docs was launched 14 years ago and was initially not seen as a strong competitor to the dominant Microsoft Office suite of business tools, but spin forward to today and Microsoft markets their 365 business suite as a cloud-based family of office tools.

Business tools and storage have become popular as cloud-based services because no local infrastructure is required and users can usually just pay as they use the services. It's so simple that nobody would return to the old days of having to buy individual software licenses that need to be installed on every laptop.

But how come the customer service industry hasn't moved with the times?

Most contact centers charge out their services using the Full-Time-Equivalent (FTE) formula, which basically means that if the call volume you are proposing means that the CX company needs 500 agents to service you, then you are going to be charged for those 500 salaries.

Then those 500 people are hired, trained, and start working 8-hour shifts in a contact center regardless of whether they are really utilized effectively or not. And then when the Holiday sales come around, the contact center struggles to keep up because they just averaged the expected number of calls across the year.

Here's another idea. Put a customer service management platform in the cloud. Allow your customers to contact what is effectively a 'virtual' contact center. The platform is connected to as many remote agents working from home as you need and manages all those connections out to them.

The agents are gig workers who are offered shifts when the company needs them, so they are utilized more effectively, and they can be scaled up and down as required. If January is a really quiet month then you just reduce the agents on the system. If Black Friday goes crazy, then you ramp up.

Utilization of agents works better and you just pay for the volume of customer interactions that were managed. Comparing this to a contact center full of under-utilized agents is a bit like comparing

Microsoft's Encarta encyclopedia on CD-ROM to Wikipedia.

In addition to just paying for what you need, and having the flexibility to meet any level of business demand, even during spikes, this cloud-based customer service model is also inherently more resilient than any operation using agents on permanent shifts inside contact centers.

For proof, look at the summer of 2020. LiveXchange has been operating like normal. This customer service model can withstand almost anything your Business Continuity Planning manager can throw at it - even a global virus pandemic. As contact centers around the world have rushed to send their employees home with hastily-purchased laptops and uncertain security procedures, we have just carried on delivering great service for our clients.

You remember how Steve Jobs[1] always used to repeat points during his famous speeches, just to ensure the audience got the point? If you are designing the new post-pandemic normal for your contact center then why not also build in resilience, better utilization of agents, and the flexibility to manage business spikes? As Jobs said when launching the iPhone 1, "are you getting it now?"

CHAPTER FOUR

HOW TO MANAGE HOLIDAY STAFFING IN THE NEW NORMAL

There are times during the year when contact center volumes spike. You might be handling ten times the normal volume of customer calls at Black Friday, or just before the end of year Holiday season as the sales take off. How do you manage your customer service team so spikes in customer contact can be handled - and all the time maintaining a high quality service?

We had a look around online and the advice from advisers is fairly typical - hire more people. But who wants to create an enormous bench of talent that will be idle for most of the year? Take a look at some of these Gartner recommendations[1], which were published just over a year ago:

- Work with HR to hire and train new staff
- Pull staff from other departments

- Declare all hands on deck
- Provide information to customers with Interactive Voice Response (IVR)
- Make part-time workers full-time during a spike

This advice doesn't look like it was published a year ago. Frankly, I'd expect to hear advice like this from Mark Twain. The customer service industry been managing a global virus pandemic over the past few months and many companies are now planning a dramatically different 2021 compared to 2019, but even without Covid-19 this advice ignores some basic business realities of the twenty-first century.

Here are my three simple tips for how you can **really** manage those spikes over periods like Black Friday:

1. **Get some content out there:** most customers turn to their phone or smart speaker first when they need help. If they just bought your new product and have a problem then what information is returned when they search Google or ask Alexa for help. Make sure you have some product-specific content, especially videos, online and well tagged so they are easy to find. Customers who get the answer from YouTube will not chase your customer service team.

2. **Automate the simple stuff:** make sure your app or website has a click-to-chat option and it's always answered immediately by a chatbot. Train the chatbot to handle your 30 most common problems. That will once again help to deflect more customers from getting in touch.

3. **Work with the gig economy:** if customers are not happy with a Google search or the chatbot then they will need to speak to someone. It's not good enough to just say 'all hands on deck', you need a dedicated customer service team that can immediately scale to meet demand. This means working with skilled mature gig workers who don't expect a week full of 8-hour shifts or a long career with one company - they will come on board for a few shifts when you are busy and need their help.

We picked on the Gartner advice, but they are not alone. Most of the consultants and analysts advising on how to manage spikes don't mention any of these three points.

Think about how your customers search for help. Make it easy for them to find relevant information and if they really need to get through to an agent then allow them to do so by ensuring that you have enough people answering calls - not by transferring your marketing team onto the phones. Ensure you have the right number of professional contact center agents on those calls by working within the gig economy. Create a pool of trained agents you can call on when required.

CHAPTER FIVE

THE FUTURE OF MANAGING SEASONAL SPIKES IN CUSTOMER SERVICE

Every business has times in the year when transactions spike. Retailers always approach Black Friday, and the end of year Holidays, with caution because they know that once they get close to those dates, contact center volumes will go through the roof.

It's the same in other industries. When a game publisher launches a new game on the app store, or for a console, then customer interactions will spike. When a consumer electronics company launches a new device or runs a big marketing campaign for an existing device, interactions will spike.

How do you handle those volumes? If you don't do anything then the customer experience is going to be so awful they might never buy from you ever again, but how can you afford to have people sitting around doing nothing when call volumes are normal - just waiting for another spike to happen?

Take a look at some of the traditional advice to customer service managers[1]. We looked around at a few business journals and these three tips are typical of the normal advice on managing short-term high volumes of customer interactions:

1. **Prepare your team:** hire temporary staff and prepare the team to be busier than usual by reducing any unnecessary stress.

2. **Use call-backs:** avoid hold times by offering the customer an option to get an automatic call-back when an agent is available.

3. **Offer multiple channels:** offer additional channels, such as chat and social networks

Maybe it's just us, but we don't think that these tips actually help very much. Your team should have the support they need to avoid stress every day they are on the job, not just during busy periods. Call-backs should always be an option for customers who prefer to call and this is 2020 - customer service has been using multiple channels for a long time now.

No business can avoid these spikes. New products, marketing campaigns, and retail sales are always going to create them, so how do you really prepare your customer service team to handle them effectively? We mean REALLY prepare?

Start thinking differently about how you manage the entire customer service process. You need to think out of the box and stop imagining that customer service is the same thing as your contact center. Break out of this mindset that more people in the contact center is the only solution to spikes in business.

Most contact centers are staffed with agents that have fixed shifts - they are at the center 8 hours a day ready to take calls whether your customers are calling or not. If you could dramatically increase control over how many agents you have answering calls then you could plan for a busy period. But how do you increase the customer service team by 300% overnight when there is no more space in the contact center?

The answer is simple. You embrace the future. LiveXchange[2] allows you to take complete control of your virtual contact center. It's a software platform that agents connect to - not a physical contact center with all the restrictions and costs of managing an office. You can schedule shifts right down to the nearest half-hour that you need covered and you can offer 500% more shifts to agents on a day when you know that your new marketing campaign is about to drop. You have complete control.

The agents are all working from home. The information is all completely secure because we have been doing this for years. These agents are people who love the flexibility of working from home and signing up for the shifts they want to work - they are not contact center agents, think of them more as domain experts. They were not sent home from a contact center because of a stay-at-home order, they love working from home. They have great experience and are skilled at supporting customers.

Traditional contact centers have never managed seasonality very well. Events such as Black Friday can be planned for to a certain extent. You can think ahead and get some temporary agents into the contact center (if there is space) or augment them with some work-from-home agents. But what happens when your marketing department drops a new campaign that triples customer interactions overnight and they didn't think to let the customer service team know?

The future of managing customer service seasonality is to move beyond the contact center. Start thinking how you could build a fantastic customer experience if you could take direct control over the number of agents you have on the team at any time of the day or night. Start building a future where seasonality is no longer a problem.

CHAPTER SIX

WHY PLATFORMS ARE THE FUTURE FOR CX

Last week, Terry hosted a Zoom call with a group of industry analysts and the LiveXchange CEO, Brian Pritchard[1]. The idea was to give them an introduction to what we are doing at LiveXchange and how we feel that this really is the future for Customer Experience (CX). It was a great session and we think that we learned just as much from the opinion of the analysts as they learned about our plans for LiveXchange.

As we talked, it felt to us that many of the questions being asked were questions that would normally be directed to a contact center operator or Business Process Outsourcing[2] (BPO) company. In fact, it seemed like we were being compared to traditional customer service BPOs.

So let's start out by getting one thing really clear - **we are not a BPO**. We are helping companies to deliver a great customer experience, but we are not a BPO or contact center outfit.

We think the sense of confusion is because almost every company uses a BPO to manage their customer service processes. Back in the day a contact center might have been an internal function - the customer service team in the basement. Since then the processes have become far more complex and now if you need to offer your customers 24/7 support in multiple languages on calls, texts, chat, and social media then it's much more common to hire a BPO.

But we are not a BPO. We are a tech platform that allows companies to plan how they want their customer service to operate and then to execute that plan by facilitating agent connections to customers in the cloud. The agents can be anywhere - all working from home. You post all your shift requirements on the platform and the remote agents sign up for those shifts.

Our platform allows companies the ability to manage their own complex customer service requirements internally. There is no need to outsource or find a BPO that can help by providing contact centers and agents.

It's not complex. Everyone understands how Uber works. There is an army of drivers out there that have all been checked and verified by Uber. They all use the Uber platform to find customers that need a ride. They can login or out whenever they want.

Customers find a ride on the Uber platform and the platform helps those drivers to find customers. The platform helps both to find what they need.

That exactly what we are doing - the platform resembles a virtual contact center and the only real difference with Uber is that the agents sign up for the shifts that are announced by the company. This allows you to post very few shifts when you know it's quiet, like Sunday evening, and many more when you expect to be busy, like Black Friday.

Some might argue that gig workers based at home and connecting to a CX platform cannot possibly be as good as a dedicated workforce based in a contact center, but think about this from the customer perspective for a moment. When they hit the 'chat' button on an app they need help with, do they care if the agent answering the request for help is in a contact center or at home?

Agents who choose to work from home are typically older, more experienced, and they have strong domain knowledge - in fact when you are recruiting you can usually focus much more on their knowledge of your industry or products than worrying about their customer service experience - that's more easily trained than a detailed knowledge of your products.

We believe that platforms really are the future for CX. We are connecting agents to customers and replacing the function of the contact center. If companies can use a platform like ours to manage their customer service function then they don't need to work with a BPO at all - just set up the platform and manage it internally.

Not only is the platform approach better, faster, more flexible and efficient, it is almost certainly going to cost you less - precisely because you don't need to keep paying a profit margin to a BPO. Cut out these unnecessary processes and you cut out expense, without losing any quality. In fact, during stressful times like Black Friday, you should even see your customer satisfaction soaring because you don't need to hire temps to help out - you have complete control.

Platforms, not BPO. Remember that. It's something you are going to be hearing a lot in 2021. Remember, you heard it right here in this book first.

CHAPTER SEVEN

WORK FROM ANYWHERE BEATS WORK FROM HOME

When the Covid-19 coronavirus pandemic began most companies with employees based in office jobs started sending their people home. Work from home became a mantra for all professional workers who could continue to work for their employer, so long as they had a laptop and broadband connection.

But now that we are seeing the restrictions lifted, many companies are asking their employees back into the office. Some of these workers are now asking for more flexibility. They have proven they can work from home, so why not stay at home permanently or just work two days a week in the office?

This is causing endless debate in the business journals. Will the office survive?[1] What about all those sandwich bars that rely on office workers for their own revenue? How do we manage childcare if we are all working from home?

To my mind, what is more important is the people themselves. How do they feel about being told they need to work from home, regardless of whether they have enough space or not, then proving they can do it before being told to get back into the office again.

Managers making these demands are likely to see a wave of unrest. Team members are tired of being judged only on the number of hours they sit in the office, their actual achievements ignored as they are passed over for a promotion by the guy who regularly has a beer with the boss. It feels like the nineteenth century all over again - factory owners dictating the rules and not listening to any discontent.

TechCrunch recently published an article[2] titled 'Work From Home is dead, long live Work From Anywhere.' The article nicely summarized the problem facing many workers at present. They have just proven to their employer that they can be more productive when they are not micromanaged. They can avoid the commute and can get more done every day. But now employers want them all to return to the old practices?

Smart employers will realize that we are at a tipping point. Employees will no longer accept the way things were. They have seen a new path and they like the flexibility it offers. For many professionals there is literally nothing that prevents them from moving to a beach, or the countryside, and continuing to add value for their employer. A fear of change and a desire to return to 'normal' is holding back both employers and employees.

Alistair Niederer, North America CEO of Ember Group[3], recently talked about how this 'new normal' might impact the customer service industry. We were particularly struck by his description of the 'third wave' of customer service. The first was about 40 years ago when telemarketing was born. The second was the offshoring boom - the massive adoption of outsourced customer service.

On a recent podcast Alistair said[4]: "This is not just affecting customer service - for every company, flexible working is now massive. It's here to stay. It will be the new way that you need to operate your business. This is the third wave for CX."

He added: "I believe this flexibility means that working from home will merge with a gig approach using GigCX platforms, like a kind of Uber for CX. Where are all those people going to reside? They can be anywhere and this transition from 'we do it all ourselves' through to outsourcing and now through to a far more flexible CX model involving work from home and the gig economy is a massive change."

Alistair's vision is timely. We are not witnessing a temporary experiment in working from home. Professionals have seen that they can work more flexibly and they can remain productive. The move to work from home customer service will not smoothly transition back to contact centers, because the customer and employee expectations have both changed. GigCX combined with work from home is going to be the immediate wave to surf, then who knows where all this flexibility will take us? Certainly not back to the office and the management practices of 2019.

CHAPTER EIGHT

GIGCX IS COMING AND IT'S BETTER THAN ANYTHING YOU HAVE SEEN

It's 2020; everyone understands the gig economy now. It's become so ubiquitous that we often see journalists using the word 'Uber' as a verb, like that company was 'Ubered' by a new market entrant.

Most people also understand that the gig economy adds something more than just a reduction in cost. We don't use Uber just because it is cheaper than a taxi, it's because the entire experience is so much better. Why would I want to walk several blocks in the rain waving at taxis when I can just ask an Uber to pick me up right here? I use Airbnb because I want to experience the use of an entire apartment when I am traveling, rather than just using a hotel.

This is well known, but then take a look at the customer service industry. Some companies, like LiveXchange[1] have been exploring the GigCX model for years, but it's still not really understood very well. Sometimes I'm asked, aren't you just moving all those agents over to a gig model so they can get paid less than they would get in a contact center?

The short answer is no, but here is the longer answer and it goes back to my point about well-known gig economy services. Often they are cheaper than the alternative, but the customer focuses on the value, not the cost. These services offer much more than just a lower price - I'd always use Uber over a traditional taxi, even if they charge similar prices.

OK, so here is the point. Traditional contact centers have seen their business model blown apart by the Covid-19 coronavirus pandemic. All their agents needed new equipment so they could work from home. New communication software and training was also needed just to keep the show on the road. Half of these people suddenly forced to work at home admit that they aren't taking security very seriously[2] because the boss isn't watching.

There are also some underlying faults in the system. Many of these people don't want to work at home - they don't have enough space or privacy to handle customer calls. They are still being managed and monitored as if they are in the office[3]. How would you feel about your webcam snapping photos at random times just to prove to the boss that you are in front of your computer?

Most of these companies have evolved as contact centers and working from home was discouraged, mostly because of security concerns. They have no culture in place to remotely manage people even if they have bought some Zoom or Teams licenses.

Which brings us back to the GigCX argument. It's obvious to us that this is not just about cost reduction. When we bring new agents onto our platform we know:

- They want flexibility
- They want to work from home
- They have the space and privacy to work from home
- They want to be paid by what they deliver, not for hours sitting at their desk being constantly monitored in case they take a bathroom break without permission
- They want to use their expertise to help people

This last point is really important. We find that the agents joining our platform are generally older than most contact center agents. They have more life experience and often have domain expertise in several areas. They are far more likely to have their own home. They are far more likely to seek out a customer service role that allows them to engage in a subject they are interested in.

Contrast all these points with the typical contact center agent. Young, not really motivated by a customer service job, often unable to work from home because there is no space.

Now think about the GigCX model. If you are building a customer service operation for a fashion retailer then why not hire people who love fashion, understand the business, and love your brand - people who are already customers and want to get paid to help others?

The gig economy works in CX and it is going to be as transformative for this sector as Uber was for yellow taxis in New York City. Contact centers containing thousands of agents all on an 8-hour shift are the yellow taxis. GigCX is coming to change this industry just like Uber and Airbnb did to theirs in the past.

CHAPTER NINE

GIGCX OFFERS A PATH TO THE FUTURE OF WORK

Employees are only productive when they have their body in a seat, at a desk, in an office. This is probably one of the most outdated and destructive concepts in modern management and yet it has persisted right up until the forced period of work-from-home (WFH) activity because of the Covid-19 pandemic.

When managers were forced to try a new type of people management they found that it works. One of the largest companies in the world, Siemens[1], has now announced that they are completely reframing their global management strategy around this recent experience[2]. Not only will they focus the activities of the entire company on permanent WFH, but they will also focus management attention on output and delivery - discarding the idea that more time at the desk must equal more productivity.

Siemens get it. The world has changed. People want more flexibility from their work. They want work that can fit around their own life. This might mean that they have caring responsibilities, or they are semi-retired and just want to work for a few hours each day. Every individual is different and companies must finally recognize this.

Globally there are millions of people employed in customer service roles. Most of them were sent home by their employer during the crisis. WFH was proven to work and customer service agents even became more productive at home - freed from long commutes and office interruptions. Most of these people[3] don't want to return to the office 100% of the time.

Research by 5th Talent in Canada on over 4,000 agents in 7 countries[4] found that most agents appreciate the flexibility they get when working from home - in particular how their managers judge them more on what they achieve than on hours worked. It's what you deliver, not who you know, that counts when everyone is working from home.

Blending a gig economy approach, that everyone knows from brands such as Uber and Airbnb, with customer experience (CX) leads to what analysts are now calling GigCX. This promises to create an entirely new type of CX that is better for the agents, better for the customers, and better for the company requiring a customer service team.

Why is GigCX so impressive? We have been talking about it throughout this book, but we will break it down further over the next four chapters.

We will focus on four key areas where we believe managers with a customer service responsibility need to appreciate the value of GigCX.

1. **Cost:** compare the cost of a chauffeur driven car taking you anywhere you want to go with the Uber app on your phone. Do you really need to pay huge upfront costs for a vehicle and then ongoing fixed costs for the car and driver or would you prefer to just pay for a car service when you need to use it? Why isn't CX like this? Why don't companies just pay for agent utilization when the agents are actually working for them? By only paying for productive agent time it's possible to dramatically reduce your total customer service cost, but also to improve the reward to agents by paying them for delivery - not just a fixed amount for an 8-hour shift.

2. **Agility:** GigCX allows customer service operations to easily manage business seasonality without the need for panic or stress. Black Friday strikes fear into the heart of many retailers because it's difficult to expand contact center operations temporarily. A GigCX approach makes this simple - and the ramp down is also simple.

3. **Flexibility:** modern customer service must be resilient. You need to mitigate risk by

delivering service from multiple locations, away from a single office, preferably across several geographic regions - or even countries. Building this flexible resilience is simple to organize with a GigCX solution. The equivalent solution with a Business Process Outsourcer (BPO) would require a network of contact centers in multiple countries.

4. **Transparency:** take control over your customer service processes. If you can directly manage a virtual contact center in the cloud with your remote agents all plugging into the service as and when needed, then why outsource these processes to a customer service provider or BPO? Everything you need can be delivered in a single, simple platform. You can take back control.

As the management of Siemens observed, managing a remote distributed workforce is very different to the processes used to manage a team inside an office. The team member spending longest at their desk is not necessarily the most productive, and may even be the least productive. Covid-19 was like shock therapy for many companies because they realized that they can be more productive by giving their employees the flexibility to work from home without managing their hours.

Modern management measures output - not hours at the desk - and GigCX adopts these principles completely. Clients working with GigCX agents only pay for productive customer engagement - nothing else. No contact centers, and no shifts where the agents are idle.

We are on a mission to inform every customer service executive globally that GigCX has arrived. Recent research by Limitless and the Ember Group[5] suggests that by 2025, 20-50% of also customer service activities will be gig economy roles. GigCX can offer dramatic improvements to your CX strategy by improving cost, agility, flexibility, and transparency.

CHAPTER TEN

THE GIG ECONOMY TRANSFORMED THE COST OF HOTELS AND TAXIS - WHY NOT CX?

Fixed costs. They are a problem for every business. Hotel chains have big, expensive buildings to maintain. Retailers have stores and stock sitting on shelves. Customer service companies have enormous aircraft-hangar-sized offices called contact centers.

The cost of maintaining and operating this infrastructure has to be paid before you can start talking profit. If your business faces a lean period then you still need to pay for all that infrastructure - that's what fixed means. It doesn't change. If you aren't making enough to meet those fixed costs, then you are facing a bleak future.

Many corporate leaders have found that cloud-based services can switch a large amount of fixed cost into variable cost. Software and services, storage space on servers and processing power. All this technical infrastructure used to be purchased up front and located in the office - now most companies pay only for the storage they need as they use it.

This is why we believe that the customer service industry is facing a wave of disruption because of GigCX. Traditional contact centers have extensive fixed and ongoing costs for their buildings, power, backup systems, cleaning, and most of the agents are on 8-hour shifts. It's not very agile and it's all fixed cost - how can this be transformed into something variable and more efficient?

Think about the hotel we mentioned earlier. A hotel chain needs buildings. Buildings need to be maintained and cleaned. People need to be on the payroll to undertake all this work. All this cost has to be absorbed by your business if you want to offer a hotel where rooms can be booked by customers.

Compare that business model to Airbnb. They don't own any properties yet over 2 million people spend the night[1] in a room they booked on Airbnb every single night. A manager with a busy schedule could ask his or her company for a car and driver, or the same manager could just use Uber on a company account. Once again, it's the difference between huge upfront, and then ongoing, fixed costs or just paying for service as you need it.

The consulting firm Everest Group has predicted[2] that by next year around 25% of all customer service agents will be working on a gig platform. Companies that need to manage their customer service processes are waking up. Why pay for all those 8-hour shifts and physical contact center infrastructure when you could just pay for the customer service agents when they are helping your customers? GigCX transforms customer service operations.

Imagine if you could build a customer service strategy that did not have to finance a contact center, agents on permanent contracts and 8-hour shifts, plus all the associated support services needed to keep such a big operation on the road? What if you could pay for agents only when they are utilized in the same way as your cloud-based servers are only charged for when utilized?

GigCX makes this a reality. It's possible to hire local agents at much less than they will cost if hired through a traditional BPO or contact center and this is not about pushing rates down so the agents feel undervalued - they are doing fine and they are local to your business, not halfway around the world. The reduction in cost is because your cost to deliver customer service no longer needs to finance the infrastructure and inflexibility of traditional customer service operations.

It is possible to reduce the cost of CX and also increase the quality of the customer experience at the same time[3], but it cannot happen using the traditional business model of a contact center. It's time to learn from companies like Airbnb and Uber and to explore how GigCX could change the future for customer service - and your business too!

CHAPTER ELEVEN

HOW TO SMOOTH OUT SEASONALITY BY TAKING CONTROL OF CX

One of the biggest problems faced by any customer service manager is estimating how many agents are needed to serve the customers that are calling, texting, chatting, and sending social media messages. With some analysis it is possible to estimate the approximate levels that are required for most times of the year, but most businesses have some form of seasonal peaks that throw the normal rules out of the window.

Retailers see this every Black Friday and when the Holiday sales begin. Sports and event companies see it every time they release tickets for a new event. Restaurants are packed at certain times of the year and quiet at other times - before social distancing anyway. Auto manufacturers know that they will be quiet after the New Year and then sales will pick up again. Seasonality affects most companies to a greater or lesser degree.

This naturally affects the number of customer interactions. A retailer will see many more transactions over Black Friday and then that leads to an increased number of queries, requests for help, or even complaints.

The increase in customer engagement varies from one industry to another, but a good example of how extreme this can be is sport. We have seen major sports associations that require 30 times their normal customer service coverage just for a short period when new tickets are on sale.

How does a traditional contact center manage this? Managers can ask agents to work some overtime, pull in agents from quiet accounts to the busy ones, and hire some temporary agents, but how can a traditional operation using physical contact centers with team members on standard 8-hour shifts manage to ramp up to 30x normal capacity just for a week?

It's not possible. No matter how many temps you call, this level of seasonality is extremely hard to cope with and usually results in tricks like the IVR discouraging non-essential calls, or call-backs being arranged so the customer can only speak to the brand when an agent is available - several hours later.

Now consider how seasonality can work in a GigCX environment.

You are using a virtual contact center platform so you can decide exactly how many shifts are needed and exactly when you need those agents ready for customers. This means that you define exactly how many agents you have available at all times. You don't need to worry about space in the contact center if you want to scale up quickly to ten times your normal team size - you just do it. As soon as the spike is over you can cut back on the available shifts and ramp down as quickly as you ramped up.

That's it. Simple and effective. It even works for more complex arrangements, such as split shifts. Some companies see a morning spike and then a quiet period all day until the evening. A traditional contact center would have idle agents all afternoon. In a GigCX environment you can specify that the available shifts match with the busy periods when you need those agents utilized effectively.

If you want to build an agile customer service solution where you only pay for agents that are utilized then you need to understand GigCX. Seasonality is no challenge when you can scale up and down just by controlling how many people you need on the team - down to the nearest half hour. That's the kind of control GigCX offers - business agility in a world that is constantly changing is going to be your key to thriving in the post-Covid-19 new normal.

CHAPTER TWELVE

USING FLEXIBILITY TO BUILD CX RESILIENCE

Flexibility will be an important driver of customer experience (CX) resilience in the coming months and years. By flexibility, we mean the ability to quickly adjust the when, where, and how you are delivering customer service and how a change in strategy can dramatically improve your future resilience.

Think about a traditional customer service solution. A contact center is at the core of a traditional solution, but since the challenges everyone faced during the Covid-19 pandemic every contact center provider has created a list of recommendations and best practice.

They have probably suggested that you consider a multi-site footprint, so risk is spread across several contact centers. This can also be reduced if you are using multiple geographies, so a problem in one country will not affect your contact centers in other locations.

They may also have advised on an improved automation strategy, so more customer interactions can be handled automatically without requiring the contact center. Almost certainly, they have also recommended the use of agents working from home (WFH) so this is blended with the contact center delivery. WFH was a natural response to the quarantine period, but it is now accepted as an integral part of the post-Covid-19 business reality.

McKinsey research found that 80% of people now working at home actually prefer it to their office. 41% said they are more productive than ever before and 28% say that their present productivity is equal to before they moved into a work from home delivery model.

McKinsey suggests that companies bringing their employees back to the office need to be careful because the office environment will be very different to how it was before the pandemic. The research says[1]: "Many companies will require employees to wear masks at all times, redesign spaces to ensure physical distancing, and restrict movement in congested areas (for instance, elevator banks and pantries). As a result, even after the reopening, attitudes toward offices will probably continue to evolve."

Let's consider all the recommended flexibility and resilience-boosting actions for contact centers in turn and explore them in the context of how a GigCX approach might work:

1. **Multiple sites:** with GigCX we are hiring agents to work from home so they will naturally be dispersed. If you have 200 agents on your team then you have spread the risk across 200 sites.

2. **Multiple geographies:** likewise, if you have a preference to hire native english-speaking Americans for your customer service team then they don't all need to be physically located in the US. You could have global travelers on the team, partners of overseas ex-pats, and Americans that have just ended up living elsewhere.

3. **Improved automation:** with a central cloud-based virtual contact center acting as a hub for the agents it's easy to add additional tools, such as a chatbot that provides 24/7 first line of support - transferring to an agent only if required.

4. **Increased WFH:** with GigCX we are focused on a 100% WFH solution so there is no need to manage blended or hybrid solutions or problems like isolation - the people who choose GigCX want to be based at home - they aren't missing the office.

The industry analysts are all talking about building CX resilience in 2021. We think the only way that an organization can achieve this is by designing extreme flexibility into their customer service solution. You can build resilience by creating the possibility to access resource from anywhere at anytime.

True resilience is never going to come from trying to extend a temporary WFH situation into a long-term business solution. Design your customer service from the ground up based on GigCX principles and all the problems of hybrid WFH and contact center solutions vanish. Think GigCX for a flexible and resilient future.

CHAPTER THIRTEEN

OUTSOURCING TO A BPO IS NOT THE ONLY PATH TO GREAT CX!

A long time ago in a galaxy far, far away... CX used to be simple. That's right. If you can remember how CX looked a decade ago then you will be aware that it used to be much easier to manage interactions with customers.

Social media was only just coming onto the scene back then so the contact center was focused on voice calls and emails. In the years since then customer demand has made it necessary to also manage online chat, asynchronous messaging like Facebook Messenger and WhatsApp, and all the popular social channels - Twitter, Facebook, Instagram etc. If you are supporting customers in multiple languages then the complexity of all these channels is just multiplied.

The conventional wisdom, for at least the past decade, has been that managing CX is a specialist process. You can't manage this in-house. You need to call in the experts. This has generally been correct, because as the channels and customer expectation on service levels have increased, it has become increasingly unacceptable to manage CX in a second-rate way. The contact center and BPO (business process outsourcing) companies have thrived because their expertise in managing customers truly was needed.

This is where GigCX is a game changer.

Not only can GigCX offer a virtual cloud-based contact center supporting the multiple communication channels you need, but by working with GigCX agents you can have a fully-staffed contact center directly under your own control.

That's right. Everything the BPO does, such as running the contact center, finding the agents, training them, managing the channels, and then reporting the metrics can all be done with a virtual platform. Imagine the level of control and transparency you can achieve If you have direct control over which agents are answering calls, when they are required, and how you want them to interact with your customers.

Some CX managers we talk to are skeptical, but we like to remind them how difficult it was just 2-3 years ago to build a global video-conferencing capability inside the office. You had to get cameras and microphones installed in meeting rooms and specialist companies earned a healthy amount managing this. Now we all just use Zoom or WhatsApp for free.

We are facing the same level of development and innovation in CX. Cloud technologies are proven for services such as CRM and office automation. The Microsoft 365 business suite is entirely cloud-based and that's what we all used to call Excel and Word - essential tools that every business needed.

Just imagine if you didn't need to hire a BPO because you could build a contact center inside the cloud, set the rules and scope, set the required shifts and coverage, and then just let the agents start handling customer questions. You could watch it, control it, and change anything about the setup immediately without having to ask an account manager at another company for help.

It's time to consider not only how you can take back control of your customer service processes, but how this will allow you to reduce cost at the same time as increasing the transparency of how your customer service operation actually works.

CHAPTER FOURTEEN

CONCLUSION AND CLOSING THOUGHTS ON GIGCX

Why is GigCX such a great model for the twenty-first century customer service industry. As we have explained in this book, there are many specific reasons why it works so well, but let's address the elephant in the room - Covid-19.

Before this virus swept the world there was a strong resistance to allowing most customer service agents to work from home (WFH). Even the largest global contact center company, Teleperformance, had just about 10,000 agents working from home globally at the beginning of this crisis. That increased to more 200,000 as the pandemic took hold.

Before the 2020 pandemic, it was feared that home networks were just not secure enough for handling customer data. This view was swiftly proven wrong as every single Business Process Outsourcing

(BPO) organization sent their people home - and asked them to continue working remotely.

Not only was it safe to work from home - if you planned for a distributed network - but many employees found that they actually preferred being at home. It freed them from managers watching their back every few minutes and basing promotion decisions on presenteeism - and they could ditch the commute.

Some of those employees sent home during the midst of the crisis did struggle. There were many issues because companies failed to embrace the more transparent and trusting management culture required of a distributed workforce. If you don't trust your team in the office then you can watch people closely and schedule regular review meetings. When you can't watch over the team then untrusting managers suffered sudden paranoia and anxiety - HOW CAN I MANAGE THESE PEOPLE WHEN I CAN'T SEE THEM!?

Some people have caring responsibility and some just don't have much private space at home so home-working isn't ideal, but this is where there is such a big difference between a crisis response and a strategic decision to hire people who want to work from home.

When people make an active choice to work from home it is because they want greater flexibility in their working hours, compared to a job with 5 x 8-hours shifts every week. They want to be away from the water cooler. They aren't going to suffer from isolation or nostalgia for the old days of the office environment - they are making an active choice to work from home. They have carved out a separate workspace, or even a spare room, so they can be serious about offering a professional service from their home.

How are the major BPOs handling the post-Covid business environment? First, there is a strong focus on building resilience into their contact center services, which means spreading service across multiple offices and even multiple geographies. Second, there is a focus on finally embracing WFH as normal. Back in April the management consulting firm McKinsey was advising that one of the most important lessons of this crisis is to scale up an effective remote-working business model. The report suggests: "The days of a fully on-site or local workforce may be over."[1]

Managing a remotely distributed team is not the same as managing a team of contact center agents that are all physically together. It doesn't even make much sense to ask them to all login at 9am or to work a continuous 8-hour shift. Perhaps it made sense when they all had to commute to a contact center, but when the commute is removed why continue to maintain the same working pattern as 19th century mill workers?[2]

CX has to enter the twenty-first century. Even the traditional BPOs now accept that they need to offer blended solutions that combine office-based workers with WFH. Some are even exploring how to build more flexibility into the working day by allowing agents to jump between accounts throughout the day, rather than focusing a shift on a single brand or account.

GigCX takes our combined experience of BPO and contact centers and builds a solution that is virtualized and cloud-based - possibly the most resilient way to plan customer service in future. But GigCX is not just about moving beyond the contact center as a delivery model for customer service, there are several specific benefits for the GigCX workers that are not available in any traditional customer service roles.

Let's consider just a few of these benefits here:

- **Diversity:** many more diverse groups of people can be included when hiring GigCX workers. The only real criteria is whether the worker knows about the products they need to support and can interact well with the customers. So the physically disabled that find it difficult to commute, or the anxiety sufferer that hates working all day everyday, can all be welcomed onto the team. Older professionals with great life experience can use their knowledge without the usual prejudice many workers face when they are approaching - or beyond retirement age. Parents can juggle caring responsibilities and work only when it suits them. If you remove the commute and fixed 8-hour shift then many valuable and skilled people can be welcomed back to the workforce.

- **Advocacy:** GigCX workers will often choose a role based on the product or brand they will represent - so they are often fans of the brand. Think about gamers that can now get paid to support other gamers or gadget geeks who love fixing complex problems with consumer electronics. By creating the ability to select gigs with a brand you can actively seek fans of the brand - anywhere.

- **Flexibility:** for decades people have sought a better work/life balance. Workers have been chained to their office, suffering long commutes and constant supervision. Managers have prized presence over delivery and only now are workers able to start demanding a more flexible working environment that embraces WFH. The virus proved that it was possible and now almost no company will ever be the same again. GigCX embraces a flexible working environment from the outset. Flexibility is in the DNA of the GigCX mindset.

- **Transparency:** one of the most common reasons why people quit their job is a lack of trust or autonomy[3]. If your boss micro-manages everything you do and is constantly critical of perceived mistakes then a common reaction is to walk away - it's usually easier than waiting for a new boss. In a GigCX environment workers know exactly what is expected, what success looks like, what they need to do and when. There is complete transparency around objectives and targets and with everyone working remotely there is a strong sense of trust - you prove your worth to the wider team by contributing your own deliverables, not just sitting at a desk.

- **Mobility:** if your partner gets a great job offer in a new part of the country you just move. If you decide you want to live by the beach and surf every morning then you just move. Society has spent decades - or longer - thinking about work as a place that we need to live close to. Suburbs and rail networks were created around this very idea. What if we can detach the workplace from work. Where would you live if you could choose to live anywhere and work remotely?

The world of work is changing. The gig economy has many critics, usually arguing that it creates a more precarious work environment, but we don't believe that the issues faced by those working for food delivery platforms are replicated in the GigCX environment.

GigCX workers represent brands and those brands will choose who they want on the team and will then value them. GigCX workers can be rewarded at higher rates than traditional contact center agents and the brands working with them can still enjoy a lower cost to provide service to their customers, compared to hiring a BPO and having to finance a contact center and inflexible agents.

Everyone wins, including the customer that can get their call answered easily on Black Friday. The CX industry is changing rapidly. Covid-19 has been a catalyst, but these changes were already taking place. The difference is that we have now seen a decade of change in our attitudes to work - especially WFH - all compressed into 2020.

All these closing thoughts listed in this chapter are testimony to the fact that there can be a silver lining to the 2020 pandemic. Yes, it took the lives of many and caused social and economic chaos, but as we rebuild our companies and countries again we can choose to return to "normal" or to make work more enjoyable, flexible, and inclusive.

In the 2020s, we can choose GigCX.

REFERENCES

CHAPTER ONE:

The Gig Economy Is Coming For CX - And Fast!

1. https://en.wikipedia.org/wiki/Gig_worker
2. https://en.wikipedia.org/wiki/Platform_economy
3. https://livexchange.com/
4. https://www2.everestgrp.com/reportaction/EGR-2019-21-R-3349/Marketing
5. https://uktechnews.co.uk/2020/05/14/gig-customer-service-booming-during-covid-19-says-report/

CHAPTER TWO:

In-house Or Outsourced CX? Why Not Just Take Control?

1. https://www.amazon.com/Outsourcing-India-Advantage-Mark-Kobayashi-Hillary/dp/354023943X

CHAPTER THREE:

The Future Of CX Can Be Found In The Cloud

1. https://www.youtube.com/watch?v=vN4U5FqrOdQ

CHAPTER FOUR:

How To Manage Holiday Staffing In The New Normal

1. https://www.gartner.com/smarterwithgartner/are-you-prepared-for-call-center-spikes/

CHAPTER FIVE:

The Future Of Managing Seasonal Spikes In Customer Service

1. https://fonolo.com/blog/2019/08/3-ways-to-prepare-your-retail-contact-center-for-the-holiday-rush/
2. https://livexchange.com/

CHAPTER SIX:

Why Platforms Are The Future For CX

1. https://www.linkedin.com/in/brianpritchard/
2. https://en.wikipedia.org/wiki/Outsourcing#Business_process_outsourcing

CHAPTER SEVEN:

Work From Anywhere Beats Work From Home
1. https://www.bbc.com/news/business-52467965
2. https://techcrunch.com/2020/05/18/work-from-home-is-dead-long-live-work-from-anywhere/?guccounter=1
3. https://www.linkedin.com/in/aniederer/
4. https://cxfiles.libsyn.com/alistair-niederer-ember-group-riding-the-third-wave-to-a-new-normal-of-waha-and-gigs

CHAPTER EIGHT:

GigCX Is Coming And It's Better Than Anything You Have Seen
1. https://livexchange.com/
2. https://www.zdnet.com/article/cybersecurity-half-of-employees-admit-they-are-cutting-corners-when-working-from-home/
3. https://www.nytimes.com/2020/05/06/technology/employee-monitoring-work-from-home-virus.html

CHAPTER NINE:

GigCX Offers A Path To The Future Of Work

1. https://new.siemens.com/global/en.html
2. https://www.forbes.com/sites/markmurphy/2020/08/11/this-powerhouse-company-discovered-how-to-stop-the-body-in-seat-mentality-and-it-only-took-one-sentence/#14e139355577
3. https://www.mckinsey.com/business-functions/organization/our-insights/reimagining-the-office-and-work-life-after-covid-19
4. https://cxfiles.libsyn.com/brian-kearney-ted-nardin-5th-talent-we-asked-4000-agents-what-they-think-of-wfh
5. https://www.limitlesstech.com/gig-customer-service-2020/

CHAPTER TEN:

The Gig Economy Transformed The Cost Of Hotels And Taxis - Why Not CX?

1. https://ipropertymanagement.com/research/airbnb-statistics
2. https://www.embergroup.co.uk/ember-gigcx-accelerator
3. https://www.embergroup.co.uk/wp-content/uploads/2020/06/EBS-Ember-GigCX-Accelerator-UK.pdf

CHAPTER TWELVE:

Using Flexibility To Build CX Resilience

1. https://www.mckinsey.com/business-functions/organization/our-insights/reimagining-the-office-and-work-life-after-covid-19

CHAPTER FOURTEEN:

Conclusion And Closing Thoughts On GigCX

1. https://www.mckinsey.com/business-functions/operations/our-insights/customer-care-organizations-moving-from-crisis-management-to-recovery

2. https://www.wired.com/story/eight-hour-workday-is-a-lie/

3. https://b2b.kununu.com/blog/why-do-good-employees-quit-leave-their-job

APPENDIX 1

LIVEXCHANGE AS AN ENABLER OF GIG CX

August 2020 White Paper
Published by Ryan Strategic Advisory
https://ryanadvisory.com/

Customer experience management is rapidly evolving, and successful organizations will be those that pivot quickly in order to adapt to new realities. No matter the country or the industry, there is more interest among those responsible for managing interactions with consumers to find better ways of driving the best possible outcomes in an efficient, cost-effective fashion. Simply put, old ways of managing contact centers and the agents on the front lines are finished. With more interactions being delivered by talent based in remote locations, the need for a cross-ecosystem offering that considers all aspects of the customer experience value chain is needed.

It is in this context that gig CX technology enabler LiveXchange's solution is relevant to the current contact center marketplace. As customer management decentralizes into agents' homes, there is a premium for one-stop shop capabilities that drive efficiencies and best possible outcomes. By packaging an offering that provides users with capabilities that include security & compliance, workforce management (WFM), recruitment and communication, LiveXchange is positioned at the forefront of the gig CX curve. LiveXchange has effectively replaced generic CRM with a solution that is designed for the changing face of customer interactions.

INTRODUCING LIVEXCHANGE

Company overview

LiveXchange was founded almost twenty years ago by a Canadian entrepreneur who believed in the potential of the gig-driven, remote-work model. Over the course of its evolution, LiveXchange has supported organizations across industries with their shift to home-based agents in Europe and North America, with an emphasis on helping drive the freelance, gig-based model.

What LiveXchange provides its clients

LiveXchange supports a variety of functions across the customer experience value chain. Effectively, LiveXchange provides its clients with a platform that is a one-stop shop for the core of a customer experience operation. These include:

- Recruitment and training;
- Scheduling;
- Agent management;
- Payroll administration;
- Ensuring operational security and compliance standards, and;
- Workforce management solutions.

But what differentiates the LiveXchange offering is its focus on work-at-home, with specific adaptability for gig CX. As organizations aim to adapt their customer experience around this as-a-service model, LiveXchange's offering stands out among the most relevant in the current marketplace.

ORGANIZATIONS SUPPORTED BY LIVEXCHANGE

LiveXchange supports a variety of clients across many corporate demographics. Its reach has many facets, and includes:

- **Companies with varying scales of revenue** - Many associate customer experience delivery with large-scale operations run by global organizations. Indeed, many solutions are designed exactly for this market segment. However, nothing could be further from the truth today. In fact, more small and medium-sized firms are conscious of driving the best and most efficient interactions possible, with the same need for the best KPIs as multinational operators. <u>The on-demand LiveXchange model feeds this business requirement for contact center operations of all sizes, whether they are emerging or already at large scale.</u>

- **Enterprises and BPOs** – LiveXchange is agnostic to the contact center business model. In fact, the offering has helped drive the best outcomes alongside real efficiencies in both captive and outsourced operations. In the case of the latter, third-party operators continue to face margin pressures, meaning a need to find ways of driving profitability. A similar financial challenge faces in-house operators, in the form of tightening operating budgets. Thus, the LiveXchange solution applies to both customer experience models.

Why do organizations use LiveXchange?

As one of the leaders in gig CX, LiveXchange has managed to work with some of the most important players across different sectors. But, what draws both enterprise and outsourced customer experience leaders to the LiveXchange solution? This question can be summed up in six points.

Adaptability

The reality is, today's more entrepreneurial gig delivery environment demands more than legacy CRM systems that track traditional work periods. LiveXchange has recognized this by eschewing solutions that were designed around the 4 – 8 hour shift, replacing them with ones that are managed on 30-minute increments. This is incredibly relevant for today's remote worker, who is looking for the chance to put in a full day's work but on their own flexible schedule. It also helps the contact center manager respond to this increasingly present labor reality alongside the heavy degree of seasonality that so many verticals are forced to deal with.

Agility and scalability

The gig workforce is more of a factor in customer experience management than anyone could have imagined. Talented and experienced contact center agents, especially those in a virtual setting, are more focused on working in an entrepreneurial fashion. Forward-looking organizations, including those in the small-and medium-sized category, need to take this into account. This was quantified in the most recent Ryan Strategic Advisory Front Office BPO Omnibus Survey of contact center executives, in which North American respondents from enterprises of up to $500m in revenues identified gig capabilities as a top 5 key selling point for their suppliers (tied for 5th with omnichannel capabilities).

LiveXchange has taken this in the development of its tools, providing users with the ability to quickly source and train the right number of agents for set periods of time, managing these teams remotely with the option of scaling up or down based on the needs of the organization.

Transparency

One of the most important facets of any customer management solution is the ability to gain maximum visibility across all aspects of the business' operations. LiveXchange has focused on providing this within their offering, such as:

- **Recruitment** – LiveXchange has a database of thousands of prospective candidates that an organization can draw from, identifying those best profiled to the skills requirement from the outset of the process. This saves time and resources relative to the traditional recruitment model, which requires significant due diligence.

- **Communication** – both managers and agents using the LiveXchange platform can take advantage of its ease of communication. Whether being used to cascade announcements to the broader organization, to interact one-on-one via email or in a secure group chat, LiveXchange has established a platform on the principals of information sharing and collaboration.

- **Workforce management** – one of the biggest bugbears of contact center managers in running operations is being able to source pertinent information easily and in real time. This is especially cumbersome for rapidly growing firms that need actionable data points as quickly as possible. LiveXchange has applied transparency in its reporting for WFM, by providing managers with reporting tools that are easy to manipulate across a variety of technical and performance-related fields.

Security

In today's increasingly virtual customer experience management environment, concerns over data protection cannot be overstated. In fact, the most recent Ryan Strategic Advisory Front Office Omnibus Survey indicates that among contact center decision-makers in major markets, the number one investment priority is information security, followed closely by compliance management.

LiveXchange has taken this priority into account with specific anti-fraud provisions built into its offering. Among the most important include:

- **Agent vetting** – at the heart of any secure virtual environment is screening agents for potential fraud risks. Thus, LiveXchange implements a system where prospective recruits are required to not only pass certain productivity tests, but they must also undergo police and credit checks. By identifying those that have criminal backgrounds, or that may pose a risk due to personal financial issues, fraudulent activity can be stopped in its tracks.

- **PCI compliance** – by providing agents with a secure desktop that works off the LiveXchange secure VPN, access to hard drive and locally-stored files and applications is blocked. Team members can only access work-related files in a read-only format, and they are able to use applications that are embedded in the LiveXchange Agent Access Workspace key.

AGENT EMPOWERMENT

Ensuring a stable, motivated team of agents is essential for delivering the best possible outcomes to consumers. However, keeping talent engaged is a major challenge for contact center managers, as identified in research by Ryan Strategic Advisory as one of the biggest operational challenges they face. LiveXchange has developed a number of approaches to address agent empowerment, by ensuring:

- Team members have the right skill sets to be working in a virtual customer experience environment;
- Training in both self-led and classroom environments is available and robust, in order to best manage evolving consumer needs;
- Success is recognized and rewarded;
- Communication is facilitated through easy-to-use technologies, and;
- Agents have direct input and visibility into their workday.

By providing the right balance of empowerment via processes and tools, LiveXchange focuses on long-term employees delivering the best outcomes for end-users.

COST EFFECTIVENESS

The reality for contact center operators is that managing costs is more challenging than ever. According to three-in-five executives in customer experience, as per the 2020 Front Office BPO Omnibus Survey there is a widespread feeling that budgets in 2021 will either stay flat or shrink. This means less money to spend on agent management, processes optimization and technology investment. It is in this spirit that the LiveXchange platform brings a great deal of value to operators of contact centers. This solution helps manage efficiencies. <u>By way of reducing expenses around recruitment, training, technology and lower attrition, LiveXchange has case studies demonstrating savings of up to 30% for firms that deploy this offering</u>.

CONCLUSIONS

<u>The evolution of the broader economy remains unclear, but what remains certain is that customer experience management will require executives be more nimble and responsive to end-user needs</u>. This means the best solutions to hand that will allow for higher degrees of adaptability than ever before. The LiveXchange model provides both outsourcers and enterprises with the capacity to respond to both a more remote, gig-based workforce while at the same time providing decision-makers with the

compliant, transparent and data-driven reporting they need. Moving forward, this solution's approach will be seen as the rule, as opposed to the exception in good customer experience management.

**GigCX: Customer Service In
The Twenty-First Century**

© Brian Pritchard, Terry Rybolt,
and Mark Hillary 2020

All Rights Reserved

Published by LiveXchange Books

Arroyo Grande, California

https://livexchange.com

www.ingramcontent.com/pod-product-compliance
Lightning Source LLC
Chambersburg PA
CBHW070424220526
45466CB00004B/1532